ЄCHOES
OF THE SOUL

DR. GREGORY ELAYADOM

TRUE SIGN
PUBLISHING HOUSE

Published by True Sign Publishing House

Address: G-3, HDB Arcade, Door Sanchar Nagar, Gulmohar,
Near UCO Bank, Bhopal, Madhya Pradesh - 462039
E-mail: truesignbooks@gmail.com
Website: www.truesign.in

Echoes Of The Soul

Author: Dr. Gregory Elayadom

First Edition: 2025

Dedication

This Anthology of Poems is dedicated with a heart welling up with sentiments of gratitude to all my teachers who taught me to read and write, who taught me philosophy, who taught me English Literature and finally who corrected and guided me throughout my research project.

These teachers enlightened my understanding and strengthened my faith in Man and Nature.

Authorial Note

The Poems in this Anthology, were written over a period of time in different moods and changing perceptions of life and when my mind was questioning Man's ups and downs in life, his belief in Religion, God; his relationships with his fellow beings, personal and interpersonal. My quest for finding consolation and stay in the lap of nature and my endeavour to put across my belief that what makes life beautiful is its not knowing what comes next.

I have been greatly influenced by mythology, philosophical and nature writings of many and of course my Christian upbringing; these influences could be reflected in these poems.

-Dr. Gregory Elayadom,
P.O. Payyampally,
Dist. Wayanad, Kerala, India-670646
Ph. No. +919544222004

About the Author

Dr. Gregory Elayadom is a native of Payyampally Village, Wayanad District, Kerala State, India. A retired professor of English, he holds a Ph.D. from Nagpur University.

Widely travelled, Dr. Elayadom is a renowned educationist, eloquent speaker, and also he was privileged to work as a United Nations Volunteer under the aegis of UNDP in the developing countries of Africa and Bhutan.

Dr. Elayadom now lives in the beautiful hilly district of Wayanad in the land of "God's own Country," Kerala, India.

Acknowledgments

I bow my head in thankfulness to the Almighty Who placed me in the midst of misty mountains, emerald coloured paddy fields, lakes, islands and amongst the poor children of Eritrea, the innocent and beautiful children of Bhutan and the street children of India, and my travels through many other countries that helped me to have an eye of an artist and the sensitivity of a poet to these beautiful places and people. They evoked the sensation of a moment in my mind with uncanny power which helped me to dissect the events of a moment or the implications of a glance with an almost painful insight into human disguises.

To my friend Ms. Corina Junghiatu from Romania, who graciously and readily agreed to write a Foreword to this Anthology of Poems. Ms. Junghiatu is a multifaceted personality: an author of repute, Literary Critic, Translator, Publisher of Verseum Literary Journal, and the Poetry Tribune Newspaper from Romania.

I am indebted to my parents, the late Mrs. Mary and late Mr. Scaria Elayadom, who taught me to connect with the heart as well as the mind and craft some kind of meaning to the human struggle.

I am really indebted to Late Rev. Bro. Mathew Alaxander for giving me an opportunity to work with the Montfortian Child Rights Movement, which gave me ample opportunities to understand the plight of the street children.

My wife Chanda and my sons and daughters-in-law and grand children who provide me with a conducive environment for my creative writing.

Dr. S. Suresh Kumar and Dr. T.K. Titus, both, my friends and writers of repute, who went through majority of these poems and gave their valuable comments, encouragement and appreciation also the appreciation of poet friends like Biswananda Sinha, Poetisa Esmeralda, Barbara Gramza Polska, Dr Tasneem Ustaad, Tapan Roy, Irene Riz and many others.

I am deeply appreciative of Mr. Joshua Joy for formatting the typescript.

My sincere thanks to the Publisher True Sign Publishing House Private Limited for their conscientious effort which enabled this book to see the light of the day.

Finally, I offer my thanks to you— all the readers of this book. It is because of you that I have had this opportunity to bring out this Anthology of poems and I earnestly hope that you appreciate my humble attempt.

CONTENTS

Foreword

In "Echoes of the Soul, Gregory Elayadom crafts a luminous testament to the resilience of the human spirit, a collection where poetry becomes both a mirror and a threshold, reflecting our deepest wounds while offering passage toward healing and understanding. Each verse resonates with an unmistakable sincerity, a voice shaped by experience, tempered by wisdom, and refined by an unyielding pursuit of truth.

Gregory Elayadom's poetry is at once intimate and universal. His words emerge from a profound awareness of suffering, of the marginalized, the silenced, the forsaken, but they do not linger in despair. Instead, they ascend, carrying the reader toward the redemptive power of faith, love, and solidarity. In poems like "Born on the Margins" and "Systemic Shackles", the stark realities of injustice unfold with unflinching honesty, revealing a world where oppression festers in silence. Yet, rather than surrender to bitterness, the author offers a counterpoint: a quiet yet unwavering hope that transformation is possible, that even the most fractured souls can find wholeness in compassion and unity.

What distinguishes this collection is its ability to bridge the sacred and the contemporary, drawing from the echoes of ancient lamentations while engaging with the existential dilemmas of our time. There is an undeniable spiritual undercurrent running through these verses, a dialogue with the divine that questions, wrestles, and ultimately seeks reconciliation. In "Tossed in the Whirlwind" and Beyond the Grey Horizon", we traverse the storm of uncertainty, only to find, in the end, the promise of renewal. Nature, too, plays an integral role in this poetic journey, its rhythms and cycles mirroring the perpetual flux of human existence, as beautifully illustrated in "Nature's Symphony of Love".

The poet's voice carries both the urgency of a prophet and the tenderness of a healer. He does not merely observe; he urges, he implores. He asks us not only to witness the world's suffering but to respond, to reclaim our shared humanity, to challenge complacency, to embrace the possibility of change. His call to unity in poems like "The Signs of the Times" is not an abstract ideal but a necessary act of resistance against division and indifference.

To read "Echoes of the Soul" is to embark on a pilgrimage, one that does not shy away from the dark valleys of human experience but dares to seek the light beyond them. It is a work of profound depth and beauty, offering solace to the weary, courage to the hesitant, and a vision of hope to all who yearn for meaning in a fragmented world.

Corina Junghiatu,
Bucharest,
România

Escape to the Ganges

I yearned to flee, to break the mold,

To find inner peace, and a new place to unfold.

Perhaps my stagnation, had made me ill,

And fresh breezes, could blow away the dust that settled still.

In films, they say, a change of scene is key,

To meet new people, and set the soul free.

But theirs is luxury, in special class and fine,

While I sought solace, in humble, simpler design.

I found my haven, by the Ganges' holy stream,

Where philanthropists' kindness, offered shelter and a dream.

No need for money, or a place to call my own,

In Dharamshalas, I found refuge, and a chance to atone.

In the cool waters, I immersed my weary soul,

And let the river's energy, make me whole.

Food was plentiful, or free, if I couldn't pay,

And in the simplicity, I found a brighter day.

No landlords, taxes, or thieves, to trouble my mind,

No police, no danger, just peace, I left behind.

Even in poverty, I found a strange, new wealth,

A sense of freedom, in the Ganges' gentle health.

Here, the needy, don't have to strive,

The mount comes to Mohammad, and the well shifts to where I reside.

In this sacred place, I found my peaceful nest,

And in the Ganges' waters, my spirit found its rest.

Beyond the Veil of Divinity

Buddha's wisdom whispers, "Atta Deepo Bhava",

Be enlightened within, for salvation lies in self-effort's wave.

No one shares the burden of our deeds, good or bad,

Like a fever, our karma's ours alone, not to be shared or pad.

In every age, heroes emerge, inspiring and true,

Like a neighbor's helping hand, more reliable than a thousand kin anew.

God's purpose, some say, is to make us kind and benevolent too,

But why then do we justify harm, in His name, with a "holy" pursue?

Fear of the unknown, a weakness we can't define,

May be the basis of our faith, a crutch to lean on, a divine sign.

Yet, this frailty's exploited, by those who claim to know,

Leaving us to wonder, if God's truly there, or just a concept to bestow.

Man rears children, wages wars, in the name of the Divine,

But would a loving God allow such harm, such heartless design?

Or is it just a few men's God, who fuels their hatred and spite?

Leaving the hungry, the innocent, to suffer, without a fight.

The paradox of existence, a complicated, tangled web,

Man's attempt to infuse meaning, where perhaps, there's none to be said.

If no Evil existed, would God's presence still be felt?

A question that haunts, as we grapple with the mysteries we've melt.

The Emergence of God

Life's essence is lodged, in a body of five,

Elements intertwined, with needs that come alive.

But as they interact, our desires multiply,

Opposing forces, like water and fire, clash in the sky.

Consciousness navigates, these conflicting tides,

Our needs, a single focus, at any given time, we can't divide.

Priorities must be set, and choices made with care,

For we can't ask for everything, from a single source, to share.

Thus, gods emerged, each with a specific role,

Gods of rain, air, life, and destruction, to make our souls whole.

The debate rages on, since time immemorial past,

About the need for god, a question that forever will last.

God, a supreme mediator, a unifying force so grand,

Born from humanity's failures, to explain life's mysterious hand.

Death, birth, goodness, and obstacles, we can't define,

Led to the emergence of god, a concept to make our spirits align.

But what if we awakened, our dormant mind's potential might?

Could we become the substitute, for the god we hold in sight?

India's tragedy, a wealth of knowledge, left unexplored,

A heritage so vast, its inheritors are numb, and ignore.

The privilege of the present, clouds our view of the past,

The immediate overshadows, the value that will forever last.

A remote value system, lost in the mists of time,

A treasure trove of wisdom, left to gather dust, and decline.

The Paradox of Humanity

Man's life is a paradox, a twisted, tangled thread,
Where strength and status, are measured by what's fed.
A man of means, must not walk, lest he lose his pride,
His worth is measured, by the vehicle he rides.

The higher he rises, the less he moves his frame,
His refined food, a punishment, to his internal flame.
He makes others toil, while he reaps the gain,
A silent decay, that eats away, like a slow-moving stain.

Rough fruit and food, are deemed beneath his station,
His refinement, measured by his delicate inclination.
He builds walls around him, thicker and taller still,
A fortress of solitude, where he hides his fragile will.

He amasses wealth, and privileges begged,
While others starve, and toil, with hearts that are begged.
Each one of us, is weaker, in some way,
The male, emotionally stronger, by virtue of his external
sway.

But the female's charms, are lethal, and internal too,

Misunderstood, and misjudged, by the male's predominant view.

Throughout history, her output, suffering, and contribution,

Have far exceeded, the male's, in every condition.

Yet, the male's bravery, gets the laurels, and the fame,

While the woman beams, with pride, and bears the blame.

But when she's applauded, how many males feel proud?

The man always keeps, his options wide, and avowed.

A woman's integrity, is tested, by her frigidity,

A deviation, from the norm, a testimony to her purity.

The choice is ours, to be dynamic, or to stand tall,

Integrity, or expediency, which path will we recall?

Humanity flourishes, in the alternative, we choose,

A paradox, indeed, that we must navigate, and muse.

Religion's Dark Descent

Despite the leaps of progress, man remains,
His own worst enemy, in endless pains.
From bullock carts to jets, from drums to cordless might,
Humanity's advanced, yet still, in darkness takes flight.

Religion, once a beacon, now an explosive device,
Tied to emotions, and manipulated with ease.
A political corporation, with interests to defend,
Detonating human bombs, and innocent lives to end.

Stagnation's foul stench, a hazard to mankind,
Unless the flow of progress, is freed from its bind.
A thousand years in India, yet still, it remains apart,
Due to barbaric tendencies, and a refusal to adapt and start.

Arrogance and ignorance, frustration and despair,
Prevent it from embracing freedom, and showing it truly cares.
Good features abound, but pedagogy denies,
Freedom and individuality, leaving only suppression's sigh.

Like communism, it's failed, to lift humanity's plight,

Thinking people shun it, and independent minds take flight.

Terrorism's medieval strategy, still employed with ease,

Subjugation and suppression, in an age of freedom's breeze.

A lion caged, with key buried deep,

A symbol of a faith, that's lost its way, and in darkness does creep.

The Empty Nest Syndrome

In big houses, parents stay alone,

Children far away, in distant zones.

Anxiety grips, as they face the test,

Of time and space, and the emptiness of their nest.

The bias of male and female, a whirlpool to navigate,

Challenging all, to master or abdicate.

I think of my sons, charting their own course,

Weaving their worlds, with wives and children, in a distant force.

Who'll be with me, in my hour of need?

The myth of a son, to perpetuate the family creed?

Inherit possessions, and property, and be my extended hand?

But self-centered man, cannot see beyond his own command.

He wants his children, to achieve what he couldn't gain,

But won't let them break free, from the chains that bound him in pain.

He wants them to follow, the system that held him back,

And trusts the very trappings, that stifled his own track.

Mankind's emotions, blind his reasoning, and fuel his distrust,

Making him wary, of others' capacities, and intentions unjust.

But in this cutthroat world, where individuals must thrive,

Some kill, while others idolize, their parents, and progeny alive.

The paradox of human nature, a complex web to unwind,

A dance between love and selfishness, forever intertwined.

The Paradox of Human Nature

Man, an egotist, impulsive and proud,

Breaks his own ideals, and modifies, aloud.

He expects the world to revere his every word,

While he himself, is inconsistent, and unheard.

Life is marked by change, and constant flux,

The sun, the earth, the planets, in eternal mix.

Each unique, yet interconnected, they sway,

A celestial dance, in an infinite way.

Why then, do we seek, to categorize and define,

Human identities, and compare, in a futile design?

No two souls alike, each one a work of art,

Original and unique, a masterpiece, that touches the
heart.

Yet, we indulge, in hatred's darkest night,

And play upon differences, with all our might.

The wealthiest, the proudest, the ugliest, and the worst,

May meet their match, in virtue, or in cursed.

Total satisfaction eludes us, it's true,

Can't we learn to accept our limits, and aim anew?

The paradox of life, is that we strive for what's not,

Rather than cherish what is, and the beauty that's been wrought.

Perhaps this discontent, drives humanity's stride,

Attaining the unattainable, we progress, side by side.

But why does man degenerate, when designed to thrive?

A creator's intent, for progress, and a life that survives.

Let us cease, this endless, and futile strife,

And celebrate, our diversity, in all its life.

For in our uniqueness, lies our greatest strength,

And in our differences, a beauty, that's at length.

"My God Why Have You Forsaken Me"?

On Golgotha's hill, a cry resounded
"My God, why have You forsaken Me?"
Echoes through eternity, a plea profound
From Jesus' heart, a sorrow unbound

But listen closely, for the cry remains
A haunting refrain, a timeless pain
From countless hearts, a chorus of despair
"why have we been forsaken?" echoes there
The marginalized, the oppressed, the worn
The refugee, the orphan, the forlorn
The sick, the suffering, the lost, and alone
All cry, "why have we been forsaken, left to atone?"

The silenced, the ignored, the voiceless cry
The victims of injustice, passing by
Their pleas, like Jesus', pierce the sky
"why have we been forsaken?" echoes, why?

Yet, in that cry, a glimmer shines

A bond between the divine and human lines

For in forsakenness, Jesus meets us here

Embracing our pain, dispelling our fear

In His cry, our cries are heard

In His forsakenness, our wounds are stirred

Toward healing, toward hope, toward love's pure light

Guiding us through darkness.

Easter's Profound Declaration

Easter's significance, a story to share,

Fulfills prophecies, and shows God's care.

The resurrection of Jesus, a defeat of death's might,

Celebrates salvation's hope, and shines with new light.

At the heart of Christian faith, this moment stands tall,

Demonstrating God's power, and love for one and all.

Jesus, the Son of God, confirmed in His might,

Validates His teachings, and sacrifice, a guiding light.

The new covenant, a promise to humanity's soul,

Conquers sin and death, allowing reconciliation's goal.

Redemption's concept, forgiveness through faith's embrace,

Illustrates salvation's path, and a life everlasting in its place.

Easter's not just history, but a declaration profound,

Inviting reflection, on divine grace, atonement's mystery unbound.

A beacon of hope, in today's fast-paced world outside,

Easter stands, reminding us, of love, sacrifice, and Jesus' stride.

A time for believers, to reconnect, and reflect,

On the essence of their faith, and the love that Jesus inspect.

Transcending mere commemoration, Easter's a personal call,

To experience, and live out, love, forgiveness, and compassion's standing tall.

Despite life's challenges, Easter reminds us, redemption's near,

New beginnings possible, through faith in Christ, and wiping away each tear.

Fostering community, unity, and a bond among believers strong,

Easter celebrates, the shared faith, and eternal life's sweet, sweet song.

A reflection of the past, and a vibrant expression of the present's might,

Easter's power shapes lives, and the world, in love's pure, shining light.

Lost in the Chaos of Belief

In the West, Africa, and America's shore,
Yoga, chants, and mantras echo evermore.
Kumbha Mela's crowds, a spiritual quest,
Vegetarianism's rise, a newfound crest.

But in India's heart, a different tale unfolds,
Scepticism grows, as ancient values grow old.
Young minds reject, the scriptural way,
Pride in non-vegetarianism, a new day.

Religious conflicts fade, but monotony remains,
A danger to growth, in stagnant, endless pains.
Switching sides, a weakness, a lack of faith,
The book of grand gossip, a magnified, distorted fate.

Dark Times have passed, but dissatisfaction reigns,
Ambition manipulates, the disgruntled, emotional pains.
The herd feels disturbed, as members stray,
Credibility erodes, in a chaotic, endless sway.

Onlookers feel horror, more than the sufferer's plight,

Gossipers react, with panic, in the dark of night.

Symptoms ignored, the disease spreads far and wide,

Adapting to new values, a challenge, to step inside.

Generations of traits, inherited, and passed down,

Any denomination, a structure, that imprisons, and wears a frown.

Good things can be adopted, without changing the label's name,

Consumables of cultures, a buffet, to taste, and reclaim.

Man creates problems, devotes life to solving the test,

Solving one, creates another, an endless chain, forever unrest.

Humanity progresses, stage by stage, generation by generation,

Improving, enduring, until the next iteration.

Beyond the Veil of Religion

True religion teaches us to lend a helping hand,
To stand by one another, in times of need, to understand.
But practice depends on the practitioner's sight,
Ignorant and greedy, turn it into a means of selfish might.

Some see religion as a means of division and strife,
Based on biases and inferiorities, a destructive life.
But others find solace, in its comforting shade,
A source of hope, in times of sorrow, a heart that's not afraid.

Yet, bloodshed and hatred, have marred its name,
Blind belief, has led to massacres, and endless shame.
I'm shaken by the preacher, who spoke with closed eyes,
Missing the essence, of true faith, that touches the skies.

Religion, sects, and castes, are tools of self-seeking might,
Used to carve out kingdoms, and exploit, with all one's light.
But holy men, with guns, and secret agents, too,
Stay in power, over hearts and minds, with a grip, anew.

Every system, devised by man, exploits nature's resources wide,

Exclusion, is the next step, a sad, but true, stride.

Faith grows, with personal experience, over time and space,

Impressing its essence, on genes, and the human face.

A faith, is based on a dream, of what life should be,

Growing, with each passing moment, in complexity.

A child, is born, a lump of flesh, that takes shape, and form,

Imprinting the code, with experiences, that forever will swarm.

I see no difference, in the essential traits, of one faith and another,

Perceptions differ, but the heart, beats with a similar thunder.

Let's look beyond, the veil, of religion's disguise,

And find the common thread, that weaves, our shared human surprise.

Rising to the Occasion

Time and circumstance shape the man,

I once was fearless, never to disband,

Resigned from comfort, to face the test,

Friends warned of danger, but I chose to invest.

They asked if I sought to make history or fame,

I replied, "I'll win with gentleness, fairness, and a progressive flame."

A notorious place, where others failed to thrive,

Became my challenge, where I chose to survive.

How can one find treasure, without taking a stride?

How can one swim, without diving into the tide?

Ability and courage, are the keys to success,

We feel shaken, before triumph, but that's the test.

The hero leads the march, through obstacles and strife,

Showing the way, through every steep fall, and rife.

In the face of failure, he finds satisfaction still,

For having striven, with courage, and an unyielding will.

Opportunities come, once in a lifetime's span,

Not like monsoon rains, that bring forth flies and frogs in plan.

A nation rises, with its youth, who strive and sacrifice,

Not with ease, and comfort, but with courage, and a willing device.

Those who seize the moment, shine like stars in the night,

We sympathize with those who miss the chance, but not with those who refuse to fight.

For it's in the struggle, that we find our greatest might,

And rise to the occasion, with courage, shining bright.

The Invisible Salaried Man

A commodity, purchasable, and cheap,

The unemployed, a supply, to be used, and to keep.

Their price climbs down, as markets rise,

A grotesque creature, needed, yet denied, with compromised eyes.

Socialists kick, capitalists enslave,

Imperialists use, as a pawn, in a game, to crave.

No honourable place, in any system's might,

A middle-class creature, struggling, through day and night.

Basic needs unmet, yet expectations high,

From family, friends, and bosses, who pass him by.

No poet sings, no storyteller weaves,

No painter depicts, the struggles he conceals.

Leaders speak, but shed false tears,

Their fortunes built, on the backs, of all his fears.

Workers have leaders, in a competitive fray,

But the salaried man, is left, to face the day.

No messiah comes, to shield him from the storm,

For virtue's reserved, for the ruling form.

The poor's sacrifices, the masses' sufferings, unseen,

No moral drawn, from the footman's pleas, unheard, and
unclean.

The value of a man, perhaps, is what he sets,

Upon himself, in a world, that forgets.

The invisible salaried man, lost, in the fray,

A life of struggle, in a world, that's gone astray.

A Lament for Humanity

In student days, a landlord's kindness shone,
A gentleman, with heart, and soul, unknown.
"Come anytime," he'd say, with a smile so wide,
"Don't worry, expenses, till you get back on your stride."

But now, I wonder, what makes people freeze,
Their sensibilities, when others plead?
Teenagers brutalized, thrown from trains,
Mutilated, bleeding, with no one to sustain.

Have we regressed, to an animal stage?
Our march towards civilization, a futile page?
A girl assaulted, in broad daylight's gaze,
No alarm raised, by her peers, in a metropolitan daze.

A generation blind, to sense, and sensibility,
I yearn for a change, in humanity.
No prosperity, no privileges, I pray,
Just make my countrymen, sensible, cultured, come what may.

Respect human dignity, don't burn, don't hate,

Don't rape, don't plunder, in the name of faith, or fate.

The shrine priest's greed, a sanction for might,

Keeping the weaker, in perpetual bondage, without a fight.

I long for the day, when people understand,

The wheel of fortune, turned, from feudal to democratic land.

The masses' voice, louder, than the classes' sway,

Responsive to human needs, in a brighter day.

A Matter of Probity

Answer books arrived by post, a conscientious teacher's test,

Correcting, evaluating, with integrity, I did my best.

A colleague came, with wife's teacher in tow,

Seeking favors, marks to boost, but I said "No!"

With consternation, I asked them to leave,

They departed, questioning my probity, my reputation to retrieve.

But I forgot the incident, by evening's calm,

My focus shifted, to the limits of self-imposed alarm.

I pondered, in a philosophical mood,

Not anxious to excuse, but to understand, as I should.

I'm liberal with marks, encouraging the young,

A benevolent duty, to push them upwards, where they belong.

No teaching occurs, in the classroom's sterile space,

It's contrasts, controversies, that etch memories in their place.

Layers of truth, peeled back, by learners, in their own time,

Extraordinary situations, that shape their knowledge, sublime.

I'm generous, to borderline cases, I confess,

For we're whimsical, subjective, in our assessments, we must profess.

Handwriting, phraseology, margins, and more,

Influence our responses, biased, perhaps, forever in store.

But to accept, or offer, bribes, a degenerate mind,

Destructive of ethics, a nation's fabric, left behind.

Treating relationships, as business opportunities, a flaw,

I've never been wealthy, but integrity, I've always drawn.

Why invite a fall, for something immaterial, I ask?

Why dishonor, the trust, of those, who've been kind, to task?

The people have been nice, why seek unethical gain?

A matter of probity, a teacher's integrity, to maintain.

Born on the Margins

Do we ever pause to ponder and consider,

The struggle to survive, against all odds, and the futility to deliver?

A child born on the roadside, with no land to call his own,

A life of dispossession, with no place to call home.

What is this thing called "law", that favors the few?

A system that denies, the basic rights, to pursue,

A house, education, clothing, transport, admission, and more,

Leaving the marginalized, to suffer, and to implore.

Observing, overhearing, the child discovers the way,

To survive, one must dispossess, or face hunger, and dismay,

A life of suffocation, suppression, and endless night,

Born into bondage, with no freedom in sight.

We sought freedom from foreign rule, but who gained?

The powerful, the corrupt, who misappropriated, and sustained,

Their grip on power, while the marginalized suffered, and
bled,

No difference, to the elite, whether the poor are near, or
distant, or dead.

The street child's cry, falls on deaf ears,

The famished face, ignored, through all the years,

No concern, no care, just a kick, and a shove,

A life of struggle, with no escape, no love.

But then comes the duper, with a twisted guise,

Using fear, or false hope, to manipulate, and compromise,

Their dreams, not yours, but made to seem the same,

A charm, an art, that's used to play the game.

Making the impossible seem possible, and within reach,

A deception, a trick, to make you believe, and preach,

Their dreams, as yours, a false, yet convincing claim,

Galvanizing the masses, with a misleading, yet stirring
refrain.

Parallels of Existence

A slum arose, like a sudden night,
Beside my room, a stark, harsh light.
Politicians' blessings, implicit, yet clear,
Future vote banks, in squalor and fear.

This juxtaposition, a chance to explore,
Contrasting lives, on my doorstep, evermore.
I saw the struggles, the hunger, the pain,
Half of humanity, in want, in vain.

In the best of times, they shiver and sleep,
Empty stomachs, a gnawing, endless creep.
I feel miserable without morning milk's delight,
While they face darkness, even in the sun's warm light.

My room's a haven, with electric light's reprieve,
Their huts, a struggle, where shadows endlessly leave.
I cook with utensils, in a kitchen of my own,
They use earthenware, and eat from the same.

Drains and sinks, a luxury I take for granted each day,

They wade in filth, with no respite, no escape, no way.

Rain brings havoc, their huts submerged, collapsing in despair,

While I stay safe, with a roof that's sturdy, secure, and fair.

Their young girls, with loin clothes, bathe by the tree,

Unfazed, unbothered, with a joy that's carefree.

I crave tongue ticklers, to make life bearable and bright,

They find solace, in half-satisfied hunger's pale light.

We forget, they're our countrymen, our own flesh and blood,

Part of our social fabric, yet left in the mud.

We boast of concern, for humanity's plight,

But neglect the struggles, of those in plain sight.

A Lifelong Quest

As a seeker of truth, I wandered and roamed,

A graduate student of philosophy, lost and unsure of my home.

Spiritual quests, like mythical tales, I was told,

Lead to deeper understanding, and a new way to unfold.

I yearned for change, to pierce the boundaries of my soul,

To find what lies beyond, and make my heart whole.

I sought unity, love, and peace, a balanced life to live,

Treasures found at the end of a spiritual journey to give.

With doubt, pain, and questions, I started my search for meaning,

Why is the world the way it is? What is eternal Truth revealing?

Does God exist? What do I believe? How much can I embrace?

Alternate realities, and the nature of the divine, I couldn't erase.

Literature and nature became my solace, my guiding light,

Teaching and connecting with students, ignited my delight.

Now retired, aging, and still questioning, I find,

The search for meaning continues, a lifelong quest of the mind.

Systemic Shackles

In a land ruled by faceless might,

I search for answers, day and endless night.

Good people proclaim their righteous creed,

But soon find themselves in a vicious system's deed.

It's a maze with no beginning or end,

Coercing all to conform, to bend and to lend.

My questioning mind is lost in a storm,

As everyone's out to exploit, to form.

Brother cuts brother, each one on the make,

In this Holy Land, where greed's at stake.

The peasant toils, with tensions his heart doth bear,

Failing to reap enough, with no one to care.

When crops are good, prices are manipulated still,

The middleman's curse, a timeless, wicked will.

He hires the skilled, and manipulates with ease,

Designating himself master, leaving others on their knees.

All business thrives on the weak and the honest too,

Throwing crumbs to the toiler, while pocketing the rest anew.

This is how the gangsters' conglomerations rise,

In urban settlements, where only the cunning survive.

No one asks how wealth's amassed, in such a short span,

For that's the unwritten law, among birds of the same clan.

Tossed in the Whirlwind

In uncertainty's whirlwind, I'm tossed and torn,
Shaken and stirred, my soul forlorn.
I wonder, where's the peace, in humanity's stride?
Is it lost in the storm, where progress resides?

Man's nature is to waste, when secure and at ease,
But every new dawn brings revolution's breeze.
It shatters the old, and lays a new foundation strong,
For in destruction's ashes, a new order takes its song.

Why fear change, and cling to the familiar past?
Why must new opportunities be built on shaking hands
at last?
Why perpetuate the self, and idolize the few?
Let future generations decide, who's worthy, and who's true.

No one takes wealth, or goodwill to the grave,
Yet, we're seduced by glory's illusion, and ancestral waves.
Each one must earn their own attainments, and rise or
fall alone,
On merit, not privilege, or circumstance, unknown.

Let's not pity, but sympathize with those who struggle and stray,

For arrogance is looking down, and rubbing salt in their wounds each day.

The wretched know their own flaws, and bad luck's heavy chain,

Let's lift them up, not tear them down, and call ourselves humane again.

The Tragedy of the Unborn

Why bear children, only to see them slain?
Why bring forth life, to be ravaged and in vain?
Women unaware, until conception's revealed,
Then, a conspiracy unfolds, a life unsealed.

A pure, innocent soul, helpless and alone,
Destroyed, discarded, without a voice to atone.
The mighty republic supports this heinous deed,
Facilities and experts, a perpetual creed.

A hundred thousand hands, backed by millions strong,
Smother and trample, a life that could have shone.
We, a degenerate species, self-centered and cold,
Each thinking only of ourselves, our hearts grown old.

What drives this butchery, this destruction of a part?
Is it fear of overpopulation, a shrinking heart?
We thrive in community, our basic instinct true,
Yet, we justify destruction, with a lie or two.

The unborn, held liable, without trial or defense,
A heinous conspiracy, against humanity's essence.
The cry of "increasing population" echoes near,
A cacophony of lies, a nation's future unclear.

Let us not be deceived, by this destructive refrain,
For in the womb, a life beats, with a future to obtain.
Let us cherish and protect, this innocent, pure soul,
For in its destruction, we lose our humanity's goal.

A Nation's Paradox

We're great when we admit our flaws and weaknesses too,
But gatherings turn to lamentations, what to do?
We bemoan the lack of chances, morals on the decline,
Depression, violence, terror, a vicious cycle's twine.

In my land, shortages mar plenty's face,
Black markets thrive, and everything's a costly pace.
We speak of kindness, values, and spiritual heights,
But principles are mere words, lost in commercial lights.

Extremism reigns, and sensitive souls despair,
Torn by dualism's treachery, with no escape to share.
The basic weakness of mind and soul, a preacher's guise,
Deceiving the world, which listens in awe, mesmerized.

If needs were basic, it would be bearable, perhaps,
But generations suffer, and self-destruction's early grasp.
A nation built on millions' pain, a freedom fighter's dream,
Lost when pampered progeny forget the struggles' theme.

Forty-Six Years of Harmony

In hills afar, we've built our nest,
Aged, yet free, with love that's truly blessed.
No expectations, no obligations bind,
Just love, pure love, that forever shines.

We've learned to cherish every fleeting day,
Invite the love we need, in our own sweet way.
Ego's whispers silenced, prejudices cast aside,
In our private world, love is our gentle guide.

We know perfection's myth, and differences are key,
Agreements don't mean uniformity.
We avoid life's crises, and don't let beliefs divide,
For us, life's beauty lies in its ever-changing tide.

God's blessings abound; we've had our share,
Qualifications, health, and love beyond compare.
This life we've lived, for forty-six years so true,
No fiction, but our story, with love shining through.

Though children grown, with lives of their own,

Their absence stirs restlessness, and hearts that atone.

But still, our love remains, a flame that burns so bright,

Forty-six years of marriage, and still, our hearts take flight.

With grandchildren's laughter, and memories so dear,

Our love's legacy lives on, year after year.

In this quiet hillside, we've built our love's nest,

Forty-six years of harmony, and a love that forever rests.

Guarding the Sanctum of Self

Speech, a double-edged sword, cuts both ways,
Freedom's paradox, in expression's gaze.
Once words are spoken, they cannot be undone,
An irreversible path, where steps are forever won.

To safeguard my convictions, I hold them tight,
Refusing to share, lest others take flight.
Their freedom to react, advise, and dissect,
Would burden me with opinions I'd rather not inspect.

Their motives differ, their understanding incomplete,
My inner world, a labyrinth they cannot greet.
The chasm between my public and private sphere,
Grows wider each day, a gap they cannot clear.

How can they truly know me, claim to understand?
A question that echoes, a mystery to withstand.
I'll guard my sanctum, my thoughts, and feelings too,
For in silence, I preserve my freedom, anew.

Embracing the Unfolding Promise

In modern times, I feel the weight of boredom's sway,
Like Scholar Gipsy, longing for a bygone day.
Excitement and inspiration seem lost in the haze,
But nature's presence reassures me, come what may.

As sunset falls, the western hills ablaze,
I watch the daylight fade, in a peaceful daze.
At life's twilight, I see a winding trail behind,
A path of actions, reactions, and the unknown's design.

My bond with nature is a bond with my own soul,
Erotic, mysterious, and whole, making me complete and whole.
Though suffering's depths may seem endless and dark,
I'll celebrate myself, just as I am, with an uncalculating heart.

In nature's lap, I'll bask with generosity and grace,
And await the promise of life unfolding in its own pace.
May interpersonal bonds and intergenerational ties flourish and grow,
And in this promise, may my spirit find its peaceful glow.

Nature's Symphony of Love

The midday sun beats down its fiery might,

Nature swoons, and all living creatures take flight.

They seek refuge from the heat's oppressive sway,

And wait for relief, come what may.

The rain-starved forests, bare and grey,

Long for the showers that have gone astray.

The hornbill's call echoes through the trees,

A melancholy sound that rustles the leaves.

But then, dark clouds gather on the eastern horizon's frame,

The winds pick up, and leaves begin to rustle and proclaim:

"A storm is coming, with rains to revive and restore,"

And the earth, like a parched babe, drinks deep once more.

The rain comes down in torrents, and the earth is reborn,

A fresh blossom explodes, and ambrosial fragrance is sworn.

The evening air is filled with sweetness and delight,

A heavenly feeling that takes flight.

The setting sun, a fiery globe in the western sky,

Bees and butterflies cling to flowers, drinking in the nectar's sigh.

I am transported to a world of emotions, pure and strong,

A realm where love resides, and my heart beats all day long.

In nature's ravishing fullness, I find my peaceful nest,

A place where love resides, and my heart is at its best.

My love orbits around her, eternally and true,

A cosmic dance of devotion, forever shining through.

Beyond the Grey Horizon

In shattered certainties, I search for truth,

A world of grey, where right and wrong are youth.

No clear distinctions, only blurred lines remain,

Sanity and madness, intertwined like a maze in vain.

I wander, lost, through this ambiguous land,

Seeking answers, but finding only shifting sand.

My mind, a battleground, where darkness and light collide,

A tryst with destiny, where reality is hard to abide.

Yet, in nature's lap, I find solace and peace,

A mysterious joy that my soul can't release.

The memories of Wayanad's landscape, pure and bright,

Haunt me, even in Bhutan's breathtaking light.

The world's contradictions, I've witnessed and known,

From Eritrea's children to Wayanad's tribal home.

The Mississippi River's waters, a life force so grand,

Echoes of Kabini river, where my childhood dreams expand.

In Salt Lake City's marvel, or Niagara's falls so high,

My spirit soars, yet shattered dreams pass me by.

Reminding me that my journey's long and unsure,

Searching for certainties, forever I'll endure.

The grey horizon stretches, a path I must roam,

Seeking truth, sanity, and a place to call home.

A Call to Unity

I follow One who bore the cross,

Humiliation and death, for love's ultimate loss.

A triumph of good over evil's might,

A beacon in darkness, shining with all His light.

I taught the youth, with dreams that knew no bounds,

Yet sorrowed that unity eluded their grounds.

I strived to emulate the One who showed the way,

Who asked the outcast Samaritan for water's sway.

He offered life-giving waters, a gift divine,

Perennial joy and life, forever intertwined.

Their ancestors suffered, humiliation and pain,

A legacy of hatred, a burden to sustain.

The high castes manipulated, divisive designs,

Preventing unity, fueling self-destructive lines.

I live amidst caste and parochial strife,

A naive tone echoing, in a gloomy, troubled life.

What can dispel the gloom, the shadows that descend?

Healing rains, nurturing life, love, and friendship to mend.

May India's timeless values, tolerance and love prevail,

Decapitating intolerance, mistrust, and the hydra's poisonous tale.

Whispers to the Divine

In nature's hush, I seek Your face,

And ask, "Why do the mighty trample the sacred space?"

Why do they crush the heart and soul of a nation's pride,

Leaving scars that time cannot hide?

Like a heart parched and yearning for a beauty rare,

I search for solace to revive a lifeless soul's care.

Will fortune smile, and circumstances align,

To guide me through life's uncertain design?

If I were to stand before Your throne,

I'd ask for waters from the well of eternal life alone.

Yet, in Your presence, words fail me still,

And I remain silent, breathing an awed silence's chill.

In the labyrinth of life's uncertainties, I roam,

Uncertain which path to take, or where to call home.

The scent of mortality wafts through the air,

And my frail humanity trembles with fear.

In this fragile state, I long to lose myself,

To find union in the bliss that transcends life's wealth.

To breathe the divine, and let go of my fears,

And in Your presence, find solace through all my tears.

Echoes of Mortality

In Wayanad's wilderness, where beasts roam free,
Life's fragile dance, a perilous spree.
My mind, a maze of messy thoughts astray,
Yearns for solace, a quiet, secluded way.

Amidst nature's mystique, I seek to breathe,
The hills, valleys, dawn, and dusk, my soul's retreat.
Though living on the edge, in uncertainty's grasp,
I'm blessed to behold this wondrous world's majestic clasp.

With every breath, I'm reminded of life's fleeting pace,
One step closer to the final, irreversible space.
Fear's dark whisper echoes, as senses start to wane,
A tear falls, symbolizing ecstasy and agony's refrain.

Obsessive compulsions, selfishness, and ego's mighty roar,
Fear the final goodbye, and the darkness that lies in store.
Another tear falls, blurring my vision, as I face the test,
To find fulfillment, contentment, and peace, before life's final quest.

A World Forsaken

In a realm where ears are closed to pain,
A world of self-absorption reigns.
Discouraging words like daggers pierce,
Slander and calumny leave hearts to freeze.

The milk of kindness has dried up and gone,
Compassion's river, once flowing, now a barren stone.
Our shadows stab, our whims and fancies bind,
A world that condemns authenticity of mind.

Dark faces of life snarl, oppressive and cold,
My exhausted mind yearns for Morpheus to unfold.
I long to rest and dream of Wayanad's gentle breeze,
Undulating beauty, a tranquil escape from life's disease.

Yet, my conscience whispers, "Where is your faith in humankind?"
A haunting question, a lingering doubt, forever left behind.

Moments Frozen

Moments frozen, timeless and bright
Ephemeral lives, in photographs' light
Emotions captured, in words that flow
Humanity's confluence, seeking solace to know

Laughter fades, leaves rustle, then cease
The house grows quiet, in a peaceful release
Forgotten dreams, in fragments remain
Pages of youth, with aspirations in vain

Yet, in the embers, a spark takes flight
Igniting a fire, that guides through the night
For in the trying, we find our way
And in the falling, we rise, come what may.

In days of yore

In days of yore when village life was sweet,

A bullock cart would rumble down the street,

Carrying farmers' wares, a symbol of their toil,

As bells on bullocks' necks tinkled like temple soil.

Like prayers rising high, dust swirled from the ground,

As villagers' hopes and dreams ascended, unbound,

The bullocks shook their heads, dissenting against the tide,

Of rulers who forgot the people, leaving them to hide.

A lift in that cart was luxury, a treasure to behold,

Like a business-class ticket, worth more than gold,

In those days of caring, sharing, and contented sighs,

Life's fleeting nature was cherished, a compromise with demise.

In reverie, I'm transported to Payyampally's shore,

Where River Kabini's waters whispered secrets, evermore,

The road wound on, a serpentine path, where bullocks would roam,

Unyoked, quenching their thirst, in harmony with nature's home.

Seventy-five years ago, life was simple, pure, and kind,

People lived in sync with nature, a symphony of heart and mind,

But now, my society's changed, values lost, rituals remain,

A nostalgic heart yearns for those bygone days, in vain.

Yet, memories linger, a bittersweet refrain,

Echoes of a time when life was lived, not merely gained,

In the silence, I hear the bells, the dust, the river's flow,

A nostalgic whisper, beckoning me back, to the village I know.

God's Self-Giving Love

On Christmas morn, we gather round,
To celebrate the Gift profound,
God's Self-Giving Love, in flesh and blood,
Jesus, the Prince of Peace, sent from above.

In darkest night, a radiant Light,
Dispels the shadows, banishes the fight,
A wider horizon of life unfolds,
As Love Incarnate, young and old.

With hearts aglow, we offer thanks,
For the Gift of Gifts, that love and peace enhances,
May this Christmas dawn, bring joy to all,
And the Prince of Peace, in hearts, forever enthrall.

May love, kindness, and compassion abound,
As we remember, God's Self-Giving Love, profound,
Merry Christmas to all, may peace and joy reside,
In the warmth of love, that Jesus, our Savior, provides.

Musings from a Hospital

Halls of Healing, Halls of Sorrow

Where life's fragile flame flickers tomorrow

A labyrinth of corridors, cold and grey

Echoing whispers of life's final day

Newborn cries, a joyful fanfare

As tiny hearts begin their life's dare

While farewell whispers, a mournful sigh

As loved ones slip beyond the twilight sky

Hope's delicate bloom, in ICU's care

Despair's dark shadows, lurking there

Loneliness, a shroud that wraps the soul

Grief's heavy chains, that make the heart roll

Wealth's gilded masks, a fragile disguise

Helplessness, a naked, pleading cry

System's cracks, a chasm deep and wide

Leaving some to face the void, with no place to hide

Sterile rooms, where life's threads are spun
And death's dark needle, weaves its final stun
The scent of antiseptics, masks the pain
As mortal fears, like specters, reign

Yet, in these halls, compassion's warm light
Illuminates the darkest, endless night
Healing hands, that soothe and mend
Comforting words, that reach the troubled end

Graveside silences, a stark reminder
That earthly glory, death's dark surrender
Riches, like autumn leaves, wither and fall
Leaving legacy, an empty, hollow call

May empathy's bridge, connect us all
And love's gentle touch, heal the greatest fall
For in life's fragile dance, we're one and the same
Bound by mortal threads, in life's ephemeral game.

The Malady of Hunger

In the depth of emptiness, a growl resounds
A chasm yawns, a void that weighs me down.
Hunger's cruel grasp, a gnawing pain
A relentless ache that refuses to wane.

Empty eyes, once bright with hope,
Now dull and sunken, a desperate scope.
Bellies ache, with agonising pain,
A constant reminder, of life in vain.

Eyes sunken, skin patched, and dry
A reflection of a soul that's lost its sigh
A search for sustenance, a quest so grand
A daily struggle, in an unforgiving land.

Future's blurred, by hunger's haze
Education's promises, in distant daze.
Opportunities lost, like autumn leaves
As hunger's chains, the mind deceives .

It stunts the young, and weakens the old
A slow erosion, of body and soul
Memories fade, like dreams forgotten
As hunger's grip, our future beholden.

But still we hope, amidst the strife
For full plates, and a nourished life
For every child, a healthy start
A world where hunger's pangs depart.

For in the depth of emptiness, a voice whisper low
"We shall overcome, for we must grow"
A resolve strengthened, by every test
A promise kept, forever find rest.

Rise against hunger's deadly might,
Break the chains, of endless night.
Let compassion guide, our every step
To wipe away, the tears we've kept.

Blossoms of Joy

In vibrant playgrounds, a kaleidoscope of wonder unfolds,

A tapestry of tiny blooms, each unique, yet perfectly curled.

Play school kids, delicate petals of diverse hue,

Unfurl their innocence, like flowers swaying anew.

Chirping laughter echoes, symphony of delight,

As birds join the chorus, singing sweet morning light.

The atmosphere vibrates with curiosity and glee,

A thousand rainbows dancing, across the sky's canvas, free.

Little hands, like tender shoots, grasp crayons and paint,

Unleashing creativity, as colours blend and taint.

Imagination blooms, like wildflowers in the sun,

As dreams and fantasies merge, forever just begun.

Tiny feet, like busy bees, moves with purpose and play,

Exploring, discovering, on this wondrous journey each day.

Smiles, like sunbeams, brighten faces aglow,

Reflecting the beauty of a world yet to know.

Teachers, gentle gardeners, nurture and guide,
Pruning doubts, watering confidence, side by side.
In this garden of learning, growth and delight,
Play school kids flourish, radiant, shining bright.

As rainbows weave their magic, across the sky's expanse,
These tiny flowers of humanity, bloom, dance and prance.
Their laughter, a melody, their joy, a treasure rare,
A garden of blossoming wonder, beyond compare.

The Signs of the Times

In the grand tapestry of human history
Every age has its own unique signature
A distinct resonance that echoes through
The corridors of time with it's kaleidoscope of complexities
Whispering secrets to those who dare to listen.
The signs of the times are etched on the walls
Of our collective consciousness to decipher.

Tempests of unprecedented fury, raging wild fires
The earth's anguish resounds like a mournful dirge
As the natural world convulses, we are forced
To confront the consequences of our choice.

In an age of fluid boundaries and shifting landscapes
Identity has become a labyrinthine puzzle curated
facades, echo chambers of ideology, politicisation
Of truth- all conspiring to fragment our sense of self.

Artificial intelligence's relentless march,
Biotechnology's promises and perils

The omnipresent gaze of the Internet of Things-
Our very existence is being redefined
As machines increasingly mirror human thought.

The widening chasm between the haves and have-nots
Systemic injustices and the erosion of empathy-
These fault lines threaten to splinter our societies
In the midst of of these converging crises
What do the signs of the times portend?
Is it the death throes of an outdated world order
Or the birth pangs of a new epoch struggling?

A call to redefine, reimagine or reboot, choose we must
To navigate this liminal space or perish.
Will we heed the warning signs and pivot towards
sustainability
And find unity amidst the shards of our fractured identity
?
And bridge the gap or succumb to the seismic forces
Of disparity or forge a new symbiosis?
The signs are not omens but opportunities
Will we heed the call or sleepwalk into a future
Shaped by the forces of inertia or champion equality?

The Forgotten Street Children

In the bustling streets of urban India
Amid the cacophony of horns and chatter
Unfolds the stark reality of street children
With eyes that once sparkled with innocence
Now reflecting the harshness of existence miserable.
Deprived of childhood joys, they navigate
The unforgiving landscape of poverty
Exploitation and utter neglect so pitiable,

Forced to flee from homes due to extreme poverty
Or ravaged by domestic violence or substance abuse
The street children fall a prey to physical , emotional
Or sexual exploitation or coerced into child labour;
With no access to formal education they struggle
To break the cycle of illiteracy and poverty.
Their fragile body a prey to malnutrition, disease
And constant struggle for survival, eroding
The self esteem, leaving emotional scars so deep.

The issues so complex, surrounding these children
Need to be highlighted and solution sought

To rescue these fragile lives without delay
By providing food, shelter and counselling
To these lives waiting to be transformed
Providing support empowering to reclaim their childhood
Nurturing a brighter future for generations to come
With empathy we can bring changes positive.

Shadows of Shame

Once pillars of strength, providers, nurturers

Now languishing in isolation, emotional desolation

Financial insecurity, neglect, malnutrition

Coupled with social indifference and familial apathy

The result of moral decay, devaluation of life and dignity.

The forgotten generation, the heartbreaking reality

Of the abandoned parents in the twilight of their years

Discarded like worn-out relics, they find themselves abandoned

When their wisdom should be cherished, love reciprocated.

Consumed by ambition and the exigencies of time

Children turn their back on parents who sacrificed themselves

For the betterment and ambition of their children.

Now hungering for human connection, love and validation;

They live in neglect, malnutrition, unsanitary conditions.

This inter- generational trauma; wounds passed down

Affecting tradition and family bonds eroding.

This shadows of shame must be faced to restore human worth

Confronting this moral failure with determination

By rekindling the flame of empathy and moral responsibility;

Enacting healthy eldercare policies by governments

To alleviate physical torture and mental anguish

Inspiring compassion, understanding and positive change.

Confronting Climate Change

The earth's fragile balance teeters
On the precipice, threatened by humanity's
Relentless pursuit of progress, so destructive
Climate change, the behemoth of environmental
Degradation and degeneration stalking our planet
Its shadows lengthening with each passing day.

Rising temperatures shatter every records
Melting polar ice caps and unleashing
Devastating natural disasters, causing
Coastal communities drown in swelling tides
While drought-stricken lands wither away
And the very fabric of ecosystems unravels
As species vanish and forests succumb to infernos.

Humanity's addiction to fossil fuels
Fuels the inferno, belching pollutants into the atmosphere
And polluting industries exacerbate the crisis.
The poor and vulnerable bear the brunt
By the consequences of climate change.

Yet hope flickers like a candle in the darkness

As renewable energy revolutionises the landscape

As solar and wind power supplant fossil fuels.

Sustainable practices transform industries

From eco-friendly agriculture to green architecture.

Together, we must rewrite the narrative of climate change

Transforming the tale of despair into

A testament to human resilience.

In War No Victor or Vanquished

I shudder even to think of another war
The dark clouds of which are looming large on the horizon.
Reflecting on the complexities of war and consequences
Is crucial for fostering empathy, understanding and peace.

The devastating consequences of wars in the past
Transcending borders, ideologies and armies
Leaving in its wake a trail of human suffering
Economic devastation, social upheavals
In varying degrees of loss and destruction.

The lives lost, families torn apart, communities destroyed
Beyond measure cannot be compensated by territorial gains.
The psychological trauma inflicted on civilians and soldiers
Lingers long after the conflict has subsided
Perpetuating violence for generations to come
To shoulder the burden of reconstruction
With resources depleted, trade disrupted
And nations pushed into instability and chaos

Hindering reconstruction and increasing economic inequalities.

Ecosystems irreparably damaged, natural resources depleted

And cultural heritage destroyed affecting survival of communities.

An eroding social fabric of nations and communities fractured

Trust shattered making reconciliation increasingly difficult.

The two world wars serve as stark reminder of war's futility

And it's lasting social and political implications on different countries.

The concept of victory in war is an illusion

Only diplomacy, dialogue and cooperation,

Can bring lasting peace, security and stability to the nations of the world.

Failure and Challenges

From the dark canvas of life's failures
The lessons learned are the scars deep
That tell a story of a brighter morrow
For in failure's shadow, we discover strength
To navigate life's labyrinth with resilience.
Let not the shadows of failure define
The outline of our soul, the lines that align
The shattered remains of dreams lie scattered
Like the crinkled faces of the village folks
Accepting with equanimity their failures.

When the weight of failures press us down
Remind ourselves "all is not lost the unconquerable will"
And rise like phoenix from the ashes of failures
To struggle to succeed with an indomitable will
Knowing failures are challenges with opportunities.

Guiding the leaky little boat, the life through
The surging billows of doubts and fears
And venture into areas never trodden before

Using this opportunity to discern our true friends

Modifying the tone and style from lessons learned

In the darkness of failure to guide us forward

And rise again from the abyss of dismal defeat

From the desolate landscape where fears converge

To a resolve to succeed from the distilled essence of experience gathered

And triumph over past defeats and failure's dark recesses

Inspiring and uplifting people to perseverance.

Know Thyself

The eternal maxim "Know Thyself"
Inscribed on the temple of Appolo at Delphi
Attributed to Socrates the great Greek philosopher
A beacon for all the Seekers of Truth and Wisdom.

An imperative, not an invitation for all
Who seek spiritual growth, wisdom and fulfillment
The foundation of personal advancement
And the way to grasp our own complex
Thought process and the meaning of life itself
The emotional complexities and desires so bewildering
That only the quest for self can reveal the depth.

Perplexed by our strength and weakness
Cultural and religious values at times at war
Our goals and aspirations real or simply imaginary
Knowing oneself will give proper guidance and vision clear.

The great religions of the world echoes this great precept:
Mindfulness and self reflection to lead to Enlightenment;

To help to dispel "Maya " to reveal the true nature of Reality or "Atman";

A daily examination of Conscience for inner peace and harmonious union with God.

The diligent practice of this great precept

Helps in understanding our goals in life

And bring inner peace and healthy relationships

Enabling to unlock the secrets of our own being

By showing "what we can do and what we cannot do"

Making all the difference in our life so mystifying.

Reconciliation

Reconciliation, the universal quest of humanity

Replete within the pages of history, religion and literature

Transcending cultural, religious, geographical boundaries

With shared wisdom on the path to forgiveness and peace

Resulting in the pursuit of harmony and fulfillment

The act of restoring relationships by forgiveness;

The vital theme reflected in all religious practices.

For the Romans their revered virtue of "clementia"

The ideal and catalyst for forgiveness and reconciliation;

While the Greek concept of "katarsis", cleanses

Individuals and society bringing inner harmony and peace.

The great seers and sages of India gave the precepts

Of "ahimsa" and "sarva-dharma-samabhav"

Which speak volumes of the power of forgiveness and reconciliation.

The cry of Jesus on the Cross was a cry of forgiveness and reconciliation

An outcry that revealed his solidarity with all the abandoned

Imploring the humankind to usher in the sparkle of radical acceptance.

This world busy reaping from where it has not sown

And beset with strife and conflicting ideas and people with colossal egos

Let the legacy of the past inspire radical change and acceptance

And their actions a beacon of hope for the sparkle of compassion

To brave the darkness and make reconciliation a living reality

In this world where all the bridges are being pulled down

Let us dance to the rhythm of life and it's mysterious ways

Weaving together a carpet from our individual threads

To cover humanity with a forgiving and compassionate love.

Life is a Puzzle Game

Life complex, paradoxical, mystifying
From birth till death like a puzzle game
An ever-challenging, obstinate mirash
Full of ups and downs, twists and turns
An enigma so difficult to comprehend;
Yet, compelled to navigate daily without fail
Through life's "meandering mazy motion"
Destined to travel with strategy and resilience.

Success and failures, joys and sorrows
Reflect in the mirror of life one after another
At times uncertainties or pleasing fulfillment
But life the puzzle is an incorrigible design
Beyond our control making it so mysterious.

Navigating this journey, the puzzle game
Which encounters challenges at every turn
Requires diligent maneuvering step by step
Solving problems that confuse and deter
With skills that establish inter-relationship

That enhances the beauty of this puzzle

Leading to success with motivation clear

Enabling the solution to the puzzling game

Unraveling life the ever-evolving mosaic.

*****

www.ingramcontent.com/pod-product-compliance
Lightning Source LLC
LaVergne TN
LVHW092019190726
843493LV00002B/503